Color Your Life

21 DAYS OF LOVING YOURSELF

PERNETHIA ARRINGTON, PMP
PAMELA ANTOINETTE, PH.D.

Tandem Light Press

Tandem Light Press
950 Herrington Rd.
Suite C128
Lawrenceville, GA 30044
www.TandemLightPress.com

Tandem Light Press paperback edition February 2016

ISBN: 978-0-9972296-0-8
Library of Congress Control Number: 201693184
THE HOLY BIBLE, NEW INTERNATIONAL VERSION®, NIV® Copyright © 1973, 1978, 1984, 2011 by Biblica, Inc.® Used by permission. All rights reserved worldwide.

PRINTED IN THE UNITED STATES OF AMERICA

This book is dedicated to those who crave a bit more color
in their lives.

ACKNOWLEDGMENTS

We would like to thank our family and friends for all of the love and support over the years that compelled us to love ourselves enough to pull this series together. We love you.

Most importantly, we acknowledge our Lord and Savior, Jesus Christ, who first loved us and showed us what it means to live a life in love. It is because of His love that we stand confidently with a pure and authentic love for ourselves so that we can effectively and unconditionally love those around us.

INTRODUCTION

Building the best things in life is as important as repairing the things that are not at their best. Coloring builds on the opportunity to meditate and focus – creating an atmosphere for mindfulness, peace, relaxation, meditation, and prayer. The *Color Your Life* coloring book series offers a creative approach to assist you in enhancing your life toward positive habits and creative life change. *21 Days of Loving Yourself* provides self-loving affirmations, the opportunity to journal, and of course, the fun of coloring and decorating your mind map toward joy.

At the starting line...

My thoughts about where I am and who I am today:

What I hope to accomplish during this 21-day journey:

Day 1

I LOVE FEARLESSLY.

There is no fear in love. But perfect love drives out fear, because fear has to do with punishment. The one who fears is not made perfect in love.

1 John 4:18

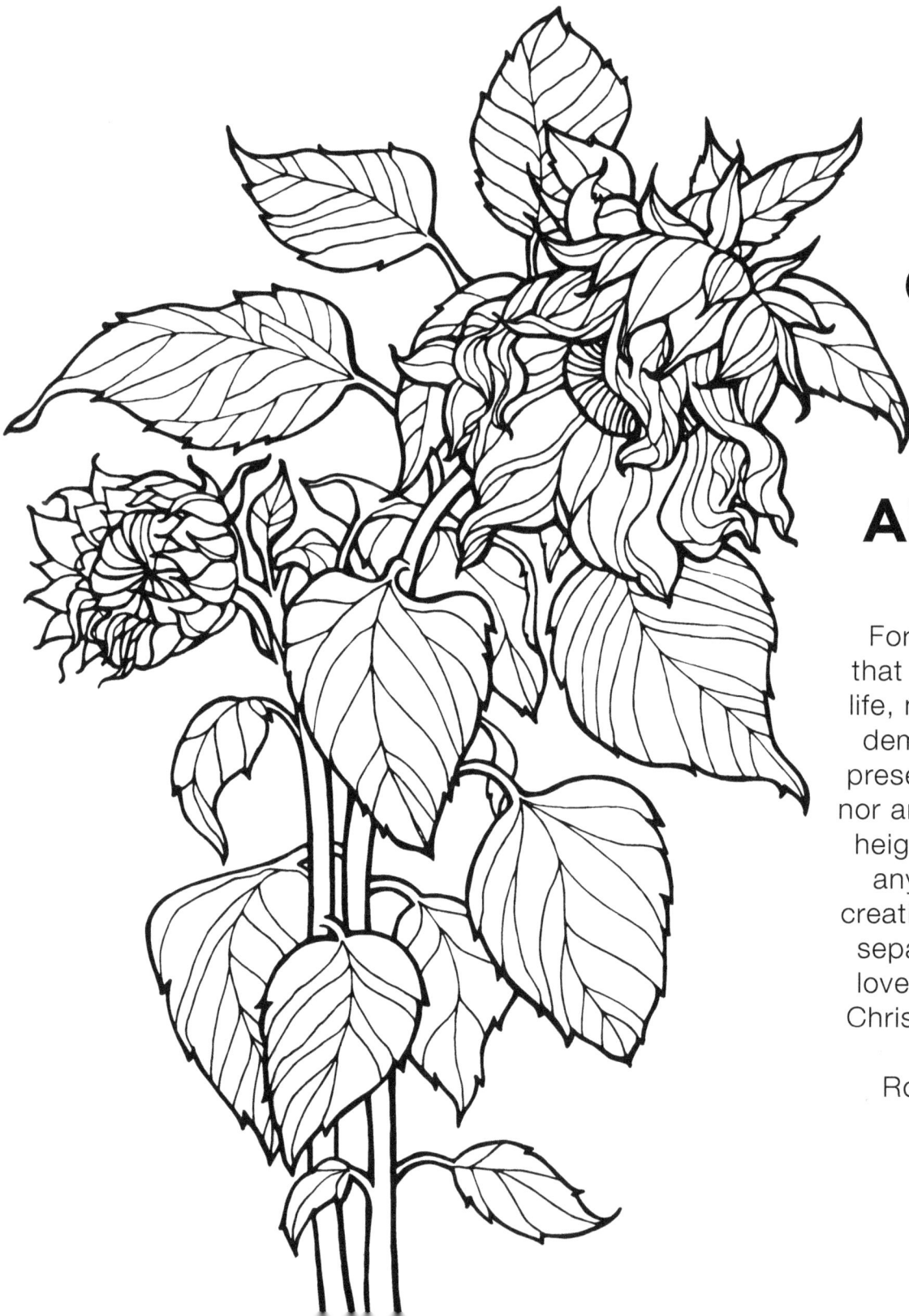

Day 2

GOD IS WITH ME ALWAYS.

For I am convinced that neither death nor life, neither angels nor demons, neither the present nor the future, nor any powers, neither height nor depth, nor anything else in all creation, will be able to separate us from the love of God that is in Christ Jesus our Lord.

Romans 8:38-39

Together Forever

I AM LOVING.

Love the Lord your God with all your heart and with all your soul and with all
your mind and with all your strength.

Mark 12:30

Mind

Soul

Strength

Day 4

I AM LOVED.

The second is this: Love
your neighbor as yourself.
There is no commandment
greater than these.

Mark 12:31

Day 5

I AM FORGIVING.
I AM FORGIVEN.

And when you stand praying, if you hold anything
against anyone, forgive them, so that your Father in
heaven may forgive you your sins.

Mark 11:25

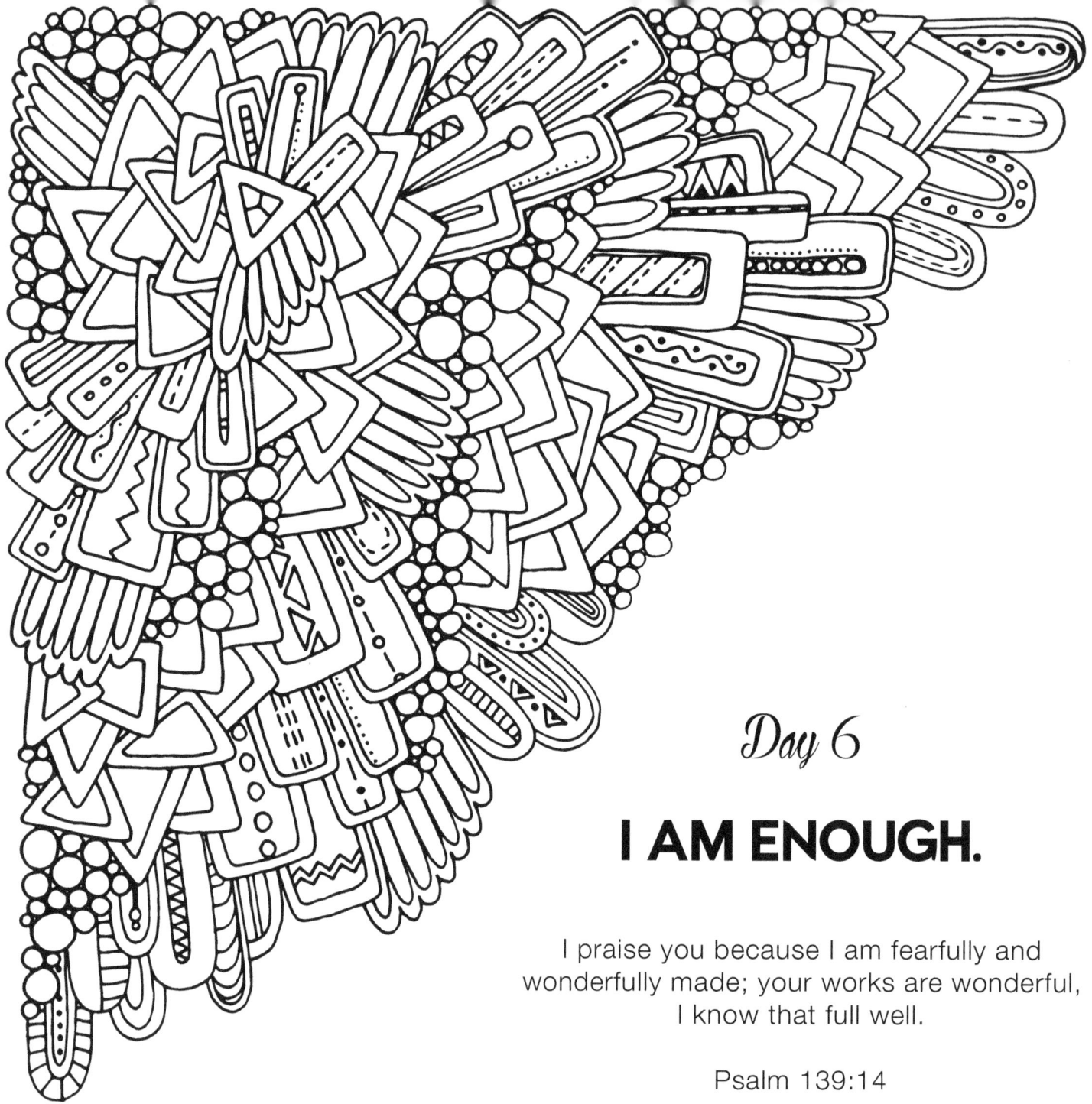

Day 6

I AM ENOUGH.

I praise you because I am fearfully and
wonderfully made; your works are wonderful,
I know that full well.

Psalm 139:14

Day 7

I AM KIND.

A kindhearted woman gains honor, but ruthless men gain only wealth.

Proverbs 11:16

Breathe

Week One Reflection

When I look in the mirror, who do I see? Who do I want this person to become?

How have I shown love to myself this week?

What was my greatest challenge this week?

What strengths do I possess that are helping me overcome this challenge?

Day 8

I AM WISE.

The wise woman builds her house, but with her own hands the foolish one tears hers down.

Proverbs 14:1

Day 9

I LOVE BECAUSE I AM OF GOD.

Dear friends, let us love one another,
for love comes from God.
Everyone who loves has been born of
God and knows God.
Whoever does not love does not
know God, because God is love.

1 John 4:7-8

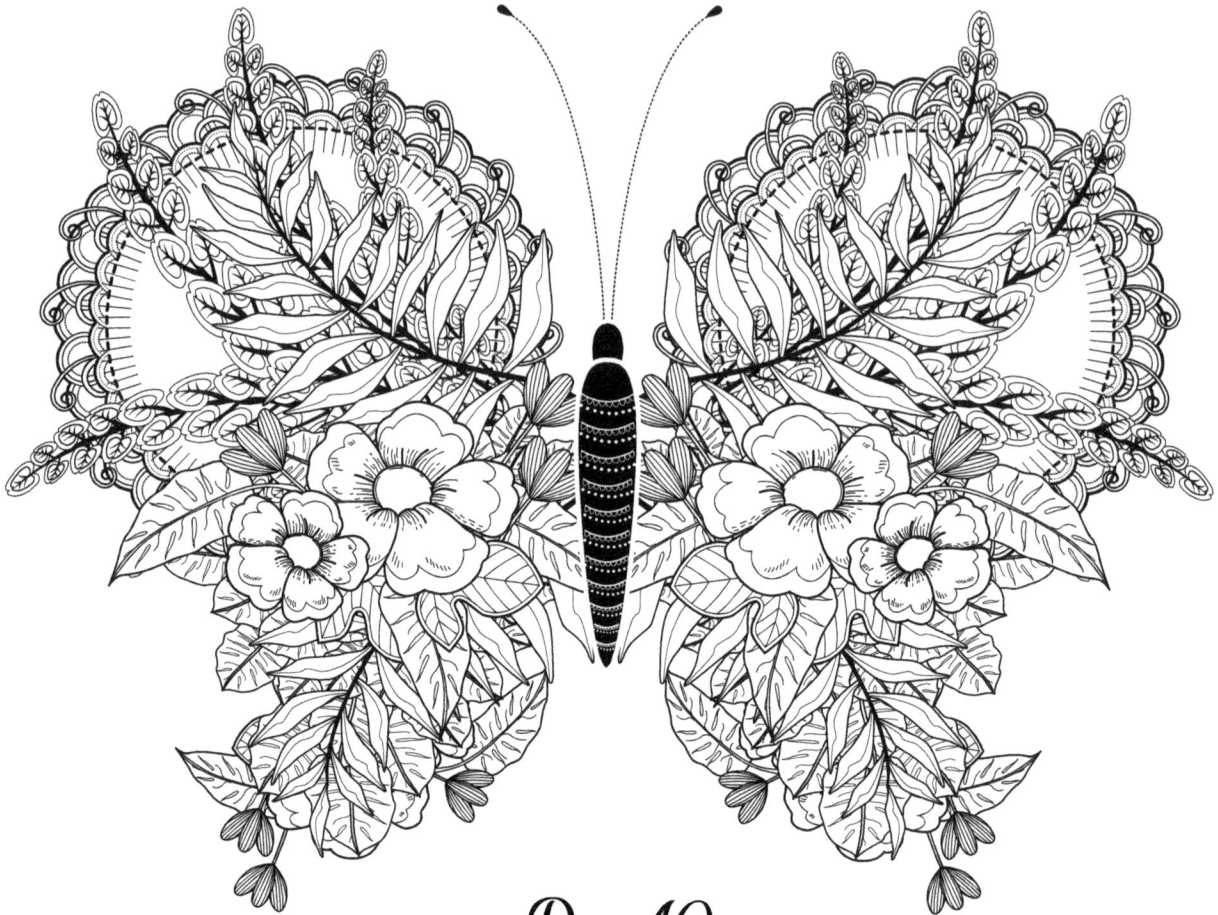

Day 10

I AM LOVE. GOD IS LOVE.

And so we know and rely on the love God has for us. God is love.
Whoever lives in love lives in God, and God in them.

1 John 4:16

I AM A TREE OF LOVE.
I AM A TREE OF LIFE.

Love is patient, love is kind. It does not envy, it does not boast, it is not proud. It does not dishonor others, it is not self-seeking, it is not easily angered, it keeps no record of wrongs. Love does not delight in evil but rejoices with the truth. It always protects, always trusts, always hopes, always perseveres. Love never fails. But where there are prophecies, they will cease; where there are tongues, they will be stilled; where there is knowledge, it will pass away.

1 Corinthians 13:4-8

Day 12

I SPEAK GENTLY TO MYSELF.

Those who guard their lips preserve their lives, but those who speak rashly will come to ruin.

Proverbs 13:3

Day 13

I SPEAK LIFE.

The tongue has the power of life and death, and those who love it will eat its fruit.

Proverbs 18:21

I AM THE PROPHET OVER MY LIFE AND FUTURE. MY WORDS ARE POWERFUL.

Since a king's word is supreme, who can say to him,
"What are you doing?"

Ecclesiastes 8:4

Week Two Reflection

How do the people in my life help me to love myself?

How have I shown love to others this week?

What are the most important characteristics about myself that remind me of my worth?

How have I shown love to myself this week?

Day 15

MY FAITH TO TOUCH HEALS ME.

But Jesus said, "Someone touched me; I know that power has gone out from me." Then the woman, seeing that she could not go unnoticed, came trembling and fell at his feet. In the presence of all the people, she told why she had touched him and how she had been instantly healed. Then he said to her, "Daughter, your faith has healed you. Go in peace."

Luke 8:46-48

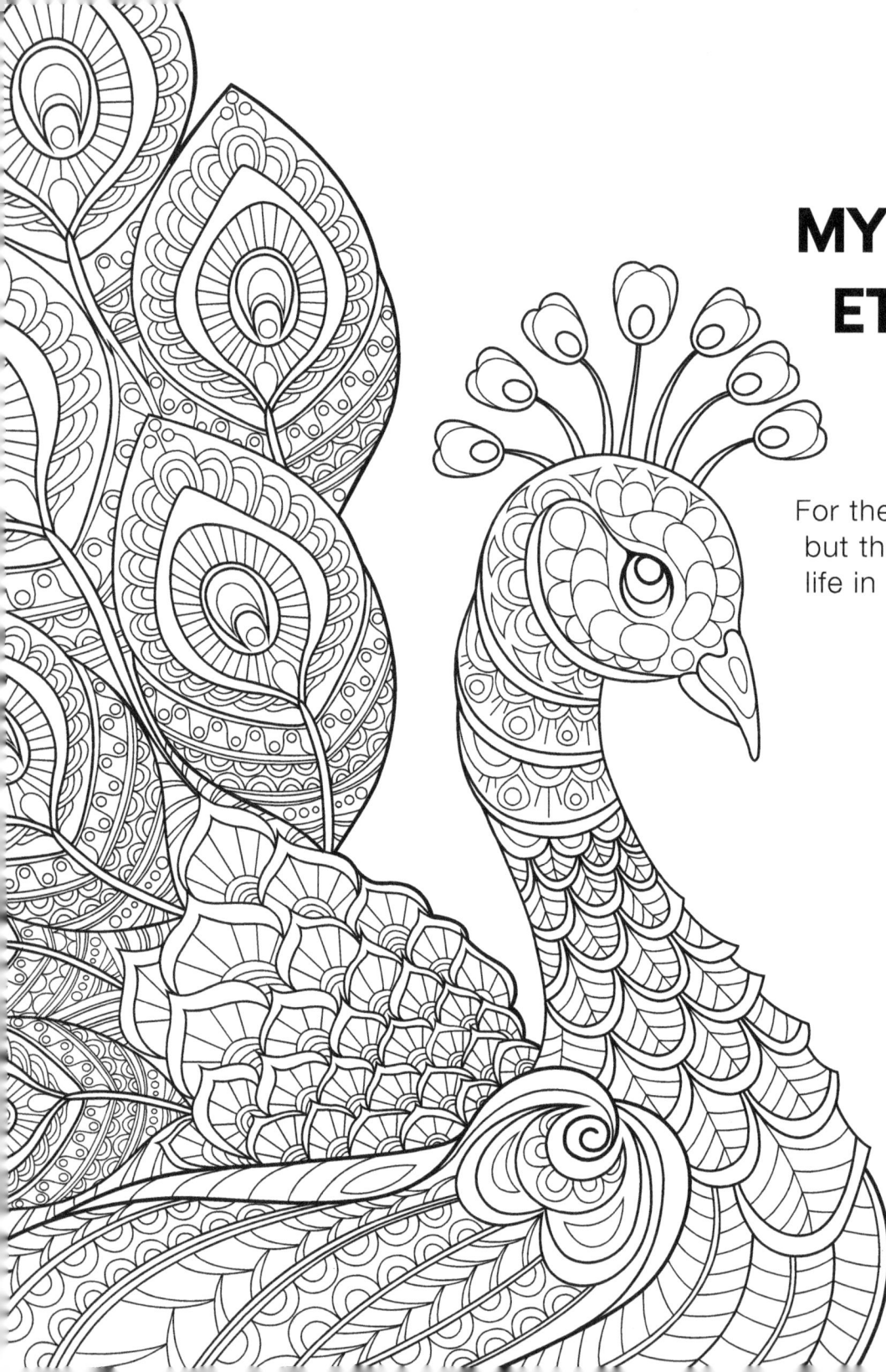

MY GIFTS ARE ETERNALLY MINE.

For the wages of sin is death, but the gift of God is eternal life in Christ Jesus our Lord.

Romans 6:23

I AM SAVED BY GRACE.
I AM SAVED BY FAITH.

For it is by grace you have been saved, through faith—and this is not from yourselves, it is the gift of God—not by works, so that no one can boast.

Ephesians 2:8-9

Day 18

I BEAR THE SWEETEST FRUITS.

But the fruit of the Spirit is love, joy, peace, forbearance, kindness, goodness, faithfulness, gentleness and self-control. Against such things there is no law.

Galatians 5:22-23

Day 19

LOVE GUIDES ME.

And now these three remain: faith, hope and love. But the greatest of these is love.

1 Corinthians 13:13

LOVE AND FAITHFULNESS ARE WITH ME ALWAYS.

Let love and faithfulness never leave you; bind them around your neck,
write them on the tablet
of your heart.

Proverbs 3:3

Day 21

I AM BEAUTIFUL.

How beautiful you are, my darling! Oh, how beautiful! Your eyes are doves.

Song of Solomon 1:15

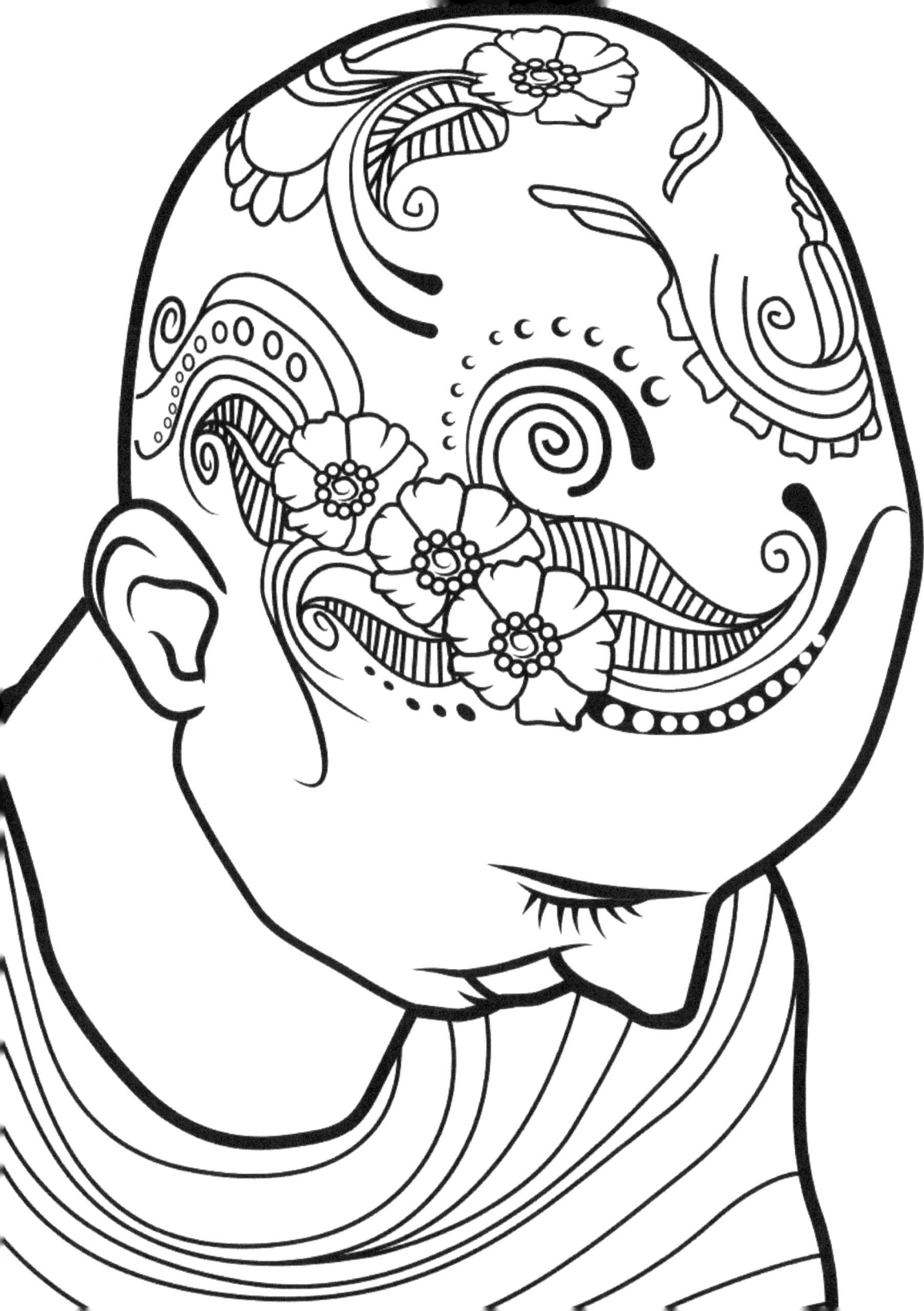

Week Three Reflection

What does loving myself mean to me?

The most enlightning part of this journey was...

How has loving myself benefited the people in my life?

How will I continue to love myself fiercely over the next 21 days?

Colorful Thoughts...

CREATE A MOVEMENT

You are peaceful, caring, grateful, mindful, kind, forgiving, forgiven, respectful, joyful, and loving. We hope that *21 Days of Loving Yourself* was as inspiring for you as it has been for us to create it. Join our community of creative life changers and share your colorful mind maps toward joy on our Instragram page: ColorYourLifeBooks. Also visit our website to learn more about new and upcoming books in this series at www. ColorYourLifeBooks.com.

What's next? Make it a family and community affair! Grab your friends, spouses, family members, and signifcant others and create a local movement of your own. Keep building in color with any of our *Color Your Life* coloring books.

ABOUT THE AUTHORS

Pernethia

Pamela

Pernethia (Penny) Arrington, PMP

Pernethia (Penny) Arrington is president and owner of Vision Speaks Coaching, a company inspired by Habakkuk 2:2-3, which states: *Write down the revelation and make it plain on tablets so that whoever reads it may run with it. For the revelation awaits an appointed time; it speaks of the end and will not prove false. Though it linger, wait for it; it will certainly come and not delay.* She is also co-founder of the Holistic Institute for Creative Life Change.

Coach Penny has a long-running history excelling as a community leader, corporate professional, student-athlete, academic scholar, mentor and coach. She instills in the organization her servant leadership style toward positive business results and expansive community impact.

Fueled by passion, Coach Penny is a pragmatic strategist who will guide visions into reality, both for Vision Speaks Coaching and its clients. Her visionary leadership is designed to build a community who also benefits from the habit of excellence and strengths demonstrated by Vision Speaks Coaching and its leadership. Coach Penny brings experience as a mentor, certified coach, accredited project management professional, program management, previous executive director of a youth mentoring organization, curriculum development, training and facilitation of one-on-one, small group, and conference-size audiences focused on personal and technical development.

Coach Penny has earned a bachelor's degree in Math from Rutgers University, the State University, a master's degree in Information Systems from Stevens Institute, a PMP from the Project Management Institute, and life coach certification from the Academy of Creative Coaching. She lives in New Jersey, is married with two children and a beloved nephew, and is a member of North Stelton AME Church in Piscataway.

Pamela Antoinette, Ph.D.

Dr. Pamela Antoinette is a certified life coach and associate professor of qualitative research at Mercer University. She holds a bachelor's degree in Journalism from Cal Poly, San Luis Obispo, a master's degree in College Student Affairs from Azusa Pacific University, and a doctorate in Leadership for the Advancement of Learning and Service from Cardinal Stritch University.

Her research focuses on interpersonal relationships, self-motivation, inspiration, resilience, and post-traumatic growth. She is the founder of Tandem Light Press, a publishing company, and co-founder of the Holistic Institute for Creative Life Change. She facilitates speaking engagements and training sessions for audiences across the country. Additionally, she has written three books, has contributed chapters to scholarly publications, and presents her research extensively for national and international audiences.

The bulk of Dr. Pamela's career has been spent in higher education, where she has twelve years of professional experience. As a student affairs professional, she received training in suicide prevention, motivational interviewing, and substance abuse counseling. After completing her master's degree in College Student Affairs, Dr. Pamela pursued her Ph.D. to better position herself to help develop leadership skills in others, particularly with the desire to help people live fulfilling, purpose-driven lives. Her vision for the Academy of Creative Coaching is that through the empowerment of the academy's graduates, they will in turn, empower the people they have the ability to touch through their coaching.

Dr. Pamela, who grew up as a member of Loveland Church in Southern California, is currently a member of New Mercies Christian Church in Lilburn, Georgia. She lives in Atlanta with her daughter while actively supporting her son, who is away at college on the west coast.

www.ingramcontent.com/pod-product-compliance
Lightning Source LLC
Chambersburg PA
CBHW061413090426

42741CB00024B/3501